T0194843

FIX THE ROOT
AND
GET THE FRUIT

GETTING UNDER THE SURFACE FOR LIFE RESULTS

JOSH STREETS

BALBOA.PRESS

A DIVISION OF HAY HOUSE

Balboa Press books may be ordered through booksellers or by contacting:

Balboa Press
A Division of Hay House
1663 Liberty Drive
Bloomington, IN 47403
www.balboapress.com
844-682-1282

Print information available on the last page.

ISBN: 978-1-9822-5913-6 (sc)
ISBN: 978-1-9822-5914-3 (e)

Library of Congress Control Number: 2020923135

Balboa Press rev. date: 11/24/2020

To my daughters. Without them, this book would have been published many moons ago. To my light worker wife for supporting me through many early mornings, late evenings, and random travels to capture my vision. To my clients and family who allowed content into this book from real-life stories and situations. Finally, to Mother Nature, for unleashing many of your secrets about our lives throughout this process. Thank you.

CONTENTS

INTRODUCTION

S ince I was a young man, I've always been curious of two things: nature and how we are connected to it and the meaning or purpose behind our lives as humans on planet earth. In a way, this book is built on a lifetime of research and experience gathered across many decades and individuals. It is my intent to address these two questions, teach how they are interrelated, and change lives in the process.

With more than 4,200 religions scattered across 195 countries at last count, this book is intended to be built on universal truths and speak to all of humanity—regardless of a chosen or unchosen faith. It is being written specifically for those who are searching for deeper meaning, those who need healing, those who are searching for purpose, and those who are just plain stuck in life. It also doubles as a guide for those who have ascended past traditional trails and are interested in helping others experience life at its fullest.

If you're reading this right now, I believe this book found you for a reason. Synchronicities and following the breadcrumbs that life tends to leave us are very important pieces of awareness. Awareness is really what this book and subject are centered around as a theme. It is about a deeper self-awareness and awareness of the world that surrounds you. It's intended to challenge what you think you know and your ways of thinking, get you more in tune with yourself, and help you understand how we sabotage or strengthen our lives based on these factors.

There will be activities that reward you with real-time success and tools to help you plan your longer-term success. These practices have been proven many times over by myself personally, my clients, and countless others across the planet. My goal was to get all this material into one location, simplify it for the masses, and make it as easy as possible to access and comprehend. I want to help people retain and leverage this knowledge and learn to teach it to others once they've used it to improve their own lives. It is a shorter guide, but that is intentional since there will be some work to do in terms of activities that lengthen the experience and help with deeper understanding and retention of the self-development work you're about to do.

You may feel an internal sense that you need to do something more to make your gift of life count. Congratulations on being alive, being willing to become more self-aware, and starting this journey. I promise that we'll go deep—and it won't be easy—but it will be worth every minute.

CHAPTER 1

OLD ENERGY VERSUS NEW ENERGY

There is a shift occurring with humanity. This awakened sense of being has been coming to fruition through various vehicles like meditation, mindfulness, wellness, and consciousness engineering. Practices that are as ancient as civilization are being modernized to heal people in today's environments, whether it's mentally, physically, or emotionally. Studies that have been done to legitimize or measure the success of these practices are numerous and similar in nature. These practices are benefiting everyone from children to senior citizens.

Whether you've practiced them yourself or are quick to naysay their benefits, you'd have to be living under a rock to not be aware of this shift. At the same time, a transition has occurred—and is continuing to occur—with the food and products we consume. Smart grocery stores, retailers, and restaurants are shifting toward healthier choices and environmental friendliness to get ahead of any potential loss in revenue spurred by consumers who awaken to the benefits of these choices. Plant-based diets and lifestyles are growing quicker than ever before thanks to confirmed links between meat and dairy and the diseases they cause. Also, an increased awareness of the effects these products have on the environment. More and more people are shifting to practices that nature has taught us, despite or possibly due to our rapid advancements in technology and culture. Health care and modern medicine are also ready for a major shift as we evolve technologically.

Internet-connected devices will eventually measure all or most of our vitals and predict or offer medical care before we even need to see our physicians. On the same front, the internet has allowed us to become a more global, connected, transparent community. This new energy happening all around us is nothing new and will continue to evolve, but much of the world is not aware of it yet. Underlying all these changes is an understanding of universal truth, of life, and of love for ourselves and the planet that continues to grow stronger by the day.

While this may seem like a modern day, tree hugging, hippy thing to say, I invite you to take a closer look at the successful people you know and how they live their lives. My guess is that you'll find them with very little fear, creating things more than consuming them, especially media, and living minimalistic lifestyles with a strong balance of travel or hobbies. They likely network with other like-minded people, dream big, get up early, read books, have a sense of meaning and a positive attitude, invest in themselves or those they trust, choose relationships carefully, are focused and driven, and make their health a priority. More than anything, they're likely disciplined and have some semblance of a routine in their lives. Many don't follow the conventional rules they've been taught; they form their own opinions, do not let beliefs limit them, and are willing to make sacrifices or take risks. They are forces of nature.

Every single one of these things defines my story and the countless stories of others, but they are not something we learned in school. Experience just means that we've messed up or have been through more in life than some others have. We all have different blueprints. I was fortunate enough to get through and learn from many of life's perceived problems prior to the age of thirty-five. I now help others try to understand the same lessons without the problems to help them make a bigger impact, quicker. It's what drives me, it's what motivates me, and it's part of my purpose or calling.

I have been likened to a modern-day shaman by some, which I'd define as one who is concerned with the health and well-being of the entire community and has access to other planes in the purpose of healing others. He or she knows, as ancient ancestors knew that, everything that exists is alive. The universe is experienced as a unified whole, and the shaman partakes in the love and nature of this beautiful reality.

My entire life, up to this point, has seemingly been preparing me to live up to a greater plan, just as you are being prepared. Thanks to my countless notebooks, journals, testaments, trials, tribulations, models, and research, I am now prepared to make my point and do my small part in strengthening the shift of humanity from old energy to new energy—or dark to light, as you will see referenced throughout this book.

My goal is to get people to turn on or shine their lights brighter by getting back into tune with their lives and their callings; to find those who are longing for answers to the whispers of their souls and are trying to choose positivity over our fear-based world; and to help others shift or awaken to the work they need to do for themselves and then for others as they grow. I hope to reveal our true nature as humans, regardless of our pasts or upbringings.

I'll be referencing the tree of life metaphor that I've illustrated to guide you in getting to the root of your problems and eventually access the fruit of your life through awareness. I am not a certified psychologist, counselor, or therapist, and I do not pretend to be one. Situations and solutions differ by individual, and if this book helps even one person or makes a positive difference in their life or the lives of others, I will consider it successful.

Bronnie Ware, a palliative care nurse from Australia, spent several years working with dying people and comforting them in their final weeks of life. During that time, she collected honest conversations with these patients on what they would have done differently if they could do it all over again. At the request of her dearly loved patients, she turned some requests into writing, which eventually became a book called *Regrets of the Dying*. I found these top five reasons to be very relevant to society today as a whole:

1. I wish I'd had the courage to live a life true to myself—and not the life others expected of me.
2. I wish I hadn't worked so hard.
3. I wish I'd had the courage to express my feelings.
4. I wish I had stayed in touch with my friends.
5. I wish I had let myself be happier.

When we take the time to become aware of the ends of our lives by reflecting on these regrets, by learning from others—or simply by drafting our retirement speeches decades in advance—we gain perspective. That's the easy part. What's harder is developing the awareness, routine, and focus necessary to do something about it. We've been taught that life happens in three stages. You learn from zero to thirty years of age, you earn from thirty to sixty, and then if you're still living, you try to return something to your family or society before you pass between the ages of sixty and ninety. This is the definition of *old energy*.

That you should wait until you're old and wrinkly to start enjoying life is one of the biggest mistruths passed down from our ancestors. Most people forget that they can find happiness before retirement, but by the time they've realized this, it's too late. *New energy* debunks this myth by showing us that it's completely possible to learn, earn, and return all at the same time—many times before you even hit thirty years of age—if you're willing to abandon the rules. Millennials are starting to figure this out, but some Generation X and baby boomers consider this notion absurd.

Society is evolving at a much more rapid pace as we enter the automation age, and all the old ideals are going the way of the dodo. Prior revolutions of the industrial age and information age laid the groundwork to get us here, but new ideas backed by science, qualitative data, and technology are being created daily. Moore's law has been spot-on when it says technological advancement doubles every two years.

One interesting body of work that has caught my attention is not the advancement of artificial intelligence or robots but the work of Suzanne Simard, a forestry researcher. In her TED Talk, she explains how she came to discover the network of biological pathways underground in forests and how trees and plant life of all kinds use mycorrhizal networks, mapped like the internet, to communicate and help one another. They share water, carbon, nitrogen, and minerals, and older trees also pass on wisdom to their kin as they age, their roots die, and they eventually deplete. They are connected in most systems as a single organism, interdependent and cooperative with one another in the process, much like the way our lives are shifting and becoming interconnected across the planet in today's day and age. There are thousands of other studies on the benefits of speaking to or caring for trees, but for the sake of my point, I will transition to how this knowledge combines with earlier points to create the tree of life diagram and this book.

Let's use fruit trees as our example. Fruit farming is a billion-dollar industry that is invested heavily in the health of its crops and its production. Most fruit trees perish because of damage to their root systems, caused by issues such as wet soil, winter cold and freezing, pest infestation, or drought. Caretakers of fertile fruit trees look for signs of potential issues in the health of the trees. These signs show in the foliage, bark, branches, and trunks of the trees. A lot of time and dedication goes into healing these trees for longevity. What if we treated our lives with the same amount of detail and holistic care?

We are beginning to apply the same knowledge to ourselves in the form of automated health diagnostics, fitness trackers, wellness programs, internet support groups, and many other preventative programs, but the entire system must be balanced and the network must share information, much like the forest and the fruit trees, if we wish to thrive. This is the basis for my work in performance consulting with both individuals and businesses over the past twenty years. You must get to the root of the problems to get the fruit of the labor. It can be very easy to spot something on the surface, apply a quick fix, and then move along in today's fast-paced world. Problems you're experiencing in life are likely preparing you for what you are here for or have asked for. Until you truly learn the lesson from these problems or change your long-term actions, you'll always get what you've always got.

The tree of life model depicts the root system below the surface that feeds the self or the soul. If one of the four roots is damaged, it's likely that the others are suffering—and what's happening on the surface is a clear warning sign. The trunk represents the self, which is the being of you. It is your ego in this physical world, your spirit in the non-physical, and your overall character.

The branches of the tree represent the stages of life you can reach if you are constantly maintaining and improving your root system. They will be broken down in thirds, using a reference from Dr. Michael Bernard Beckwith. Life happens to you near the bottom branches, which is known as *victim mode*. As you become more aware, you realize that life happens *by* you which is depicted in the mid-level branches.

As you continue upward near the top branches, you find that life starts to happen *through* you for the sake of others. You become a vessel of sorts to inspire or teach others. Many people have lived their entire lives in the bottom set of branches by not having the awareness that lies within this book and within all of us if we seek it.

It was recently concluded in a series of surveys by an organizational psychologist that 95 percent of people believe they are self-aware, but only 10–15 percent actually are. Low self-awareness leads to poor mental well-being and self-destructive behaviors such as addictions. I personally have been fortunate enough to climb every single branch with exception of a few at the very top, and I recall my experiences throughout this book. However, make no mistake, I started from the bottom and was surrounded by others on the bottom for a large period of my life. The amount of empathy I feel for others, many I haven't met, is sometimes unbearable. If they could just understand that being here in this body, at this time, is a gift—despite what they are feeling or were taught as a child. This book is my vessel to heal others in the global community, connect you with each other, attempt to unblock any stuck energy you have, and continue climbing the tree of life with you and for you.

CHAPTER 2

DEFINING MOMENTS

The defining moments of my first stages of life include attending my father's funeral on my ninth birthday, growing up in a lower-class, single-parent household, marrying a sociopath, having a premature baby with complications, losing my home and everything I owned in a natural disaster, getting divorced, gaining sixty pounds of fat, struggling financially, losing a job, and becoming a single parent. However, I have somehow kept a smile on my face through it all. I have learned from every single day and used it to fuel my success. Despite these valleys, I still managed to achieve a six-figure career in my twenties, create my own company, touch numerous lives in the process, rebuild my credit, lose the weight, find my soul mate, remarry, raise a happy family, and make contributions to my community and to society.

I have not dealt with overcoming terminal illness or escaped a near-death situation, but I've experienced adversity. Is it anything that anyone else hasn't experienced? Definitely not. Is it the greatest survivor story of all time? Not even close. Yes, these are first world problems, but they are common problems that many people face in their lives that can easily alter the course of their futures if an understanding of life is not present. It requires a deeper awareness for those like me who grew up without an emotionally or financially supportive environment and had to figure it out on their own, guide themselves through the struggles, and be strong and brave. For those who don't even know where to begin or are still trying to figure it all out, get your highlighters ready.

Let's begin with our life-changing tree of life assessment to see your current views on life or awareness of the world around you. Visit www.fixtheroots.com to find the assessment and all other materials related to each chapter.

I remember the knock on our rented farmhouse door and everyone coming into the kitchen to see who it was. We lived in a very rural area and rarely had uninvited guests. To hear such a prominent knock, we knew something wasn't right. It was the county sheriff.

My mother answered the door, and my little sister and I stood behind her. My grandfather was waiting at the kitchen table; he had stopped by because my father did not meet him that morning at the time they had planned to go hunting. The sheriff explained that there had been a car accident. It was a single-vehicle crash, and it involved my father. It was a snowy day in December, and the jeep he was driving left the highway at a high speed, went into a deep ditch, and flipped after hitting a culvert. His vehicle was totaled, and he was rushed unconscious to the area hospital. He had severe internal bleeding, collapsed lungs, and the injuries were too significant to repair. He died that morning, and the sheriff was there to break the chilling news to my mother. We kids huddled behind her, and I'll never forget the things she said following that news and how her body almost crumbled there in the doorway. A few days later came the funeral—on my ninth birthday.

I'd never had so much attention in my life as that day. All of my classmates (who were willing) arrived at the funeral during school hours to support me. They came via school bus, in numbers. For many of them, it was their first funeral. For me, it was a shocking surprise.

Following the services, there was a gathering at my grandparents' house. I was showered with hugs, kisses, random birthday cards, money, and attention from strangers I had never met. That was how I'd remember my ninth birthday. It never really goes away, at least thinking about that day as a child. Even into adulthood, I allowed the what-if's to play out in my mind. What would my life have been like had he not died that morning? What if I had actually remembered the last thing he said to me or retained some really positive memories of our relationship? What if it all hadn't happened around my birthday? Would it be different or feel different? As I've grown older, I've come to terms and have accepted growing up without a father. I've seen how the problems it created for me growing up have actually helped me become the person I am today.

My mother never remarried, and growing up as the man of the household gave me an extra sense of responsibility at a young age. At twelve years old, I got a job delivering newspapers and haven't stopped working since. When it came time to pay for basketball camp, and we didn't have the money, I negotiated mopping floors before camp each day to pay my entrance fee. I grew up quick, but because of my mother being a single, full-time-working parent, there was usually no one there to cheer me on at sporting events, give me rides, or talk about the game or things that were going on in my life.

As high school began, I took my self-perceived maturity and quickly became friends with the senior class. My freshman year included parties, girls, cutting classes, and road trips. It all caught up with me in eleventh grade, and I found myself a very different young man. I was in trouble with teachers, had poor grades, had been kicked out of some sports, and was struggling to go to school. I was struggling to even get out of bed. Feelings of guilt settled in quickly. I felt like I was unable to get out of my current situation. I felt hopeless and stuck. I started worrying about living in that small town forever, getting a factory job like my family members, and never doing the things I was dreaming about—like traveling the world or doing something bigger than myself. Having a father figure there to push me or guide me may have been the best thing that could have happened to me. Instead, I received a handwritten letter from my mother expressing her disappointment—and a wish for me. She wished I would not follow in her footsteps and would go out and live up to my potential.

In my senior year, I moved beyond the guilt, hopelessness, and sadness, and I stopped being afraid. I improved my grades, got back into some sports and activities, and turned it around. I wanted to get out of my small, decaying town of five thousand people and start a new chapter. It motivated me. I had seen the victim mentality all around me, and I somehow had the instinct to rise above it. It motivated me so much so that on the day of my graduation party, I collected my gifts, packed up a vehicle, gave my mother a hug, and moved out for college. Since then, I have donated funds back to the school to allow teenagers in the alternative high school program a chance to get out of their normal lives and take a field trip to places with greater opportunity. My principal exclaimed that some students were living in rural homes with dirt floors and had never been to a shopping mall. Any funds to help provide experiences would be beneficial, she said. So I found a way to send them as I became able. I also participate in the Big Brothers program for at-risk youth to try to be the adult mentor I never had.

In my twenties, I sent an email to my crush from high school. She grew up in a nearby town, and many guys were competing for her attention. She had a cousin in my hometown and would occasionally visit during the summer. I found her email address via her college's website and thought I'd take a chance.

I received an immediate reply—thanks to AOL audibly announcing whenever someone received a new email message at that time: "You've got mail!" She was interested in driving to where I was and going on a date. Within weeks, she had decided she wanted a full-time relationship. She was involved as a contestant in Miss America pageants and seemed to have a good head on her shoulders, which would really give me bragging rights with the guys back home. I had a young man's awareness level and point of view.

Within a few weeks, she approached me about getting our own place together. I obliged since it seemed like perfect timing. I was making a decent amount of money in my leadership position, was ready to get out of the bachelor lifestyle, and had dreams of white picket fences, a yellow Labrador, and the quintessential family I never had growing up. I was a very goal-driven material-driven young man, and she shared all of my visions.

What I did not know, which I am very well aware of now, is that I would be spending more than a decade of my life in the grips of a sociopath. She was an expert at manipulation, lying, cons, and infidelity. She lacked empathy for anyone but herself, was impulsive in her behaviors, was a narcissist, and didn't have an ounce of remorse for anything she did. She had textbook antisocial personality disorder, but I was a naïve and polite young man who had no clue.

She had similar dreams, and I was just the ticket she needed at the time to achieve them. She was cunning and had a lot of practice in getting what she wanted by flashing a smile or telling a lie. She was perfectly capable of telling so many lies to others that it was difficult to keep up with—and she believed her lies at times. As long as she was charming and generous at the beginning of a relationship, she would have a chance to feel out the other person to see if there was anything she could get as a perk of the relationship. With her two best friends, she had a history of slowly preying on their lack of confidence to gain control over them without them knowing it.

With me, she preyed on my empathy. She could be outwardly calm one minute, but if I ever disagreed with her or wanted to do something by myself, drama would be created out of thin air or she would twist what I said to confuse the situation. If you challenged or confronted her, you had better look out. I remember being repeatedly punched in the face while driving for challenging her on a topic. Once, when I wanted to attend a college football game with a friend, she took all of my shoes and covered them in shampoo to thwart my leaving the house. She had very few real friends, as most sociopaths do, and I was it for her. Many outbursts led to many broken dishes, regular arguments, and a lot of stress. I also had limited interactions and networking opportunities.

She couldn't hold down a job for most of our relationship, and for some reason, I accepted that. I tried to coach her or make her better every step of the way. Many days, she could be found shopping or watching television at home. Taking care of a sociopath can be a full-time job that is disguised as a relationship.

Being distraught over finances, crumbling goals, the relationship and having a limited social life wreaked havoc on me mentally, physically, and emotionally. I gained nearly sixty pounds because of the disappointment and anger. I turned to fast food for the affordability and comfort. I was also drinking alcohol to try to cope. I was obese, had difficulty breathing while sleeping, and was constantly sick.

My close friends recognized my anguish and did not support the relationship, but I didn't see them enough for it to matter. I put my head down and continued to devote as much to my career as I could. Eventually, to help keep the relationship alive, she pressured engagement and marriage. She would change, she said, but she needed to make sure the commitment was there on my end. I scraped money together for a ring, and we got married in the same church in my hometown where her parents had gotten married.

In recent years, I have taken the time to educate people about identifying sociopaths in relationships and finding the courage to move on. The person who loves the least tends to control the relationship, and that was very evident in mine. Had I known then what I know now about this mental disease, it would have dramatically changed my reaction and the amount of time I stayed with her. I was likely put in her life for a reason—or she in mine—yet I still reflect on why. My gut says it was the potential to educate others in the same situation that I was in. If any of these traits sound familiar or you grew up with a parent with narcissism or sociopathic behavior, do yourself a favor and research the warning signs and symptoms and how to get out of it or cope with these individuals.

I was finally climbing the branches of the tree of life. I realized that life could either happen *to* me or I could take charge, and it could happen *by* me. My career was thriving, and I was regularly winning leadership awards and incentives for the performance of my teams. I lost most of the weight with diet and exercise and took some control of the relationship. I was not happy, but I had outlets in place to improve mentally, physically, and emotionally.

Leading, consulting, self-developing, reading, and achieving were my focus. Emotional intelligence, strengths finder, Myers-Briggs, DISC, Enneagram, Dale Carnegie training, and just about every other tool for awareness or improvement became my source of inspiration. At an off-site leadership retreat, I received a phone call from my wife. "Josh, it's me. I am at St. Luke's hospital for an emergency pregnancy appointment, and I'm being admitted three months early. You need to get here as soon as you can—we might be having this baby today."

What followed after that call was a diagnosis of my wife with stage 3 HELLP syndrome, a form of preeclampsia that was shutting down her internal organs. To this day, it remains a medical mystery to childbirth, but it was regulated for the next thirty-six hours with low lighting, constant vital checks, and a team of physicians and nurses. We needed every hour we could get to assist the baby's lungs in development to increase the chances of survival at birth.

Prior to my wife's organs shutting down, we went in for an emergency C-section. My daughter was born just above two pounds and was immediately transferred to the neonatal intensive care unit, and she would remain there for two months. I'll never forget spending my days and evenings there, the dark rooms, and the beeps of all the machines humming throughout the rooms. I'll never forget the worried families, infants dying in rooms next to us, the sadness, and very few smiles or joys.

Keeping my daughter's heart and oxygen rates at livable levels while preventing infections was the main focus. Keeping her alive was an around-the-clock job for the staff, and we almost lost her many times. We were informed that she would likely grow up with vision, hearing, and digestive issues due to her early birth at the twenty-eight-week mark. There were also learning disabilities that would be associated with an underdeveloped child. Midway through our stay at the hospital, her medical bill topped the million-dollar mark.

After multiple PIC lines, feeding tubes, and one very close encounter with death by not breathing for a prolonged period of time, her strength started to grow. Her heart got stronger, and she miraculously pulled through. We were able to take her home on a tachycardia monitor, at three pounds, six ounces, and had multiple trips back to the hospital for check-ups.

I was thrust immediately into fatherhood. In the first few weeks of having my daughter home, my wife needed emergency gallbladder surgery. It had failed after the birth and needed to be removed. After the procedure, she was knocked out on anesthetics and mumbling in the front seat of the car as I drove my heart monitor-connected, three-pound child and her home.

Near the end of the trip, my daughter began to choke on her own vomit in the backseat, and the heart rate monitor began beeping loudly as her oxygen supply was being cut off. Not able to rely on my passenger, I had to quickly stop in the middle of the road, put the car in park, and run around to grab the baby out of the backseat to clear the airway and sop up the vomit. I was reviving an extremely fragile burrito-sized human while trying to divert traffic from rear-ending us or our vehicle.

Situations like that seemed to follow me for the next several years, but this million-dollar baby has escaped the vision, hearing, and digestive issues once thought to surely alter her life. As far as learning complications, she is one of the smartest students in her class, and while still very thin, she is just as tall and happy as a normal child. Given the way she entered the world, this was not the expectation. Being courageous and willing to confront problems head-on is something that this experience has gifted me. I have donated to the March of Dimes to support research into premature infants, and we like to visit the NICU to try to comfort other families when we can.

Two weeks after we got our daughter home from the hospital, the next challenge presented itself. Our first home, just off the core of the downtown area of the city, was in jeopardy of flooding due to a five hundred-year flood. That type of flood is so torrential that it only has a .02 percent chance of happening in an area any given year. The rain came and didn't stop. We were evacuated from our home, infant in tow, with very little notice or time to grab our belongings. Since we were quite far from a body of water, we had very little belief that it would cause anything more than some water in the basement—until the levies failed.

We woke up the next morning at a friend's house after the forced evacuation to see video footage of our home from a passing emergency boat on *Good Morning America*. It was almost completely submerged, and the water had not crested yet. Upon my attempt to get to the home to save whatever I could, I was stopped by the National Guard troops several blocks away where the water had risen. After living in near poverty as a child, living in a trailer park, and earning my way into homeownership and nice material possessions, it was all suddenly erased. We had no flood insurance to cover the property or damages. FEMA listed the house as a complete loss, and I still owed approximately twenty-eight years of mortgage payments on it.

As the water receded and cleanup began, I entered the home for the first time. I had to force my way in the front door, which had been stuck in mud and debris inside the house. Inside was pure destruction, the rancid smell of feces from wastewater treatment facilities that had overflowed, and white mold growing all over the floor and walls. Framed pictures were covered in dried mud and grime on the ruined hardwood floors.

Every disastrous step through the home uncovered more of nature's wrath and connection to our lives. Old friends and some family members showed up to help clear all our belongings and bring them out to the curb, and the president of the United States flew in to declare the area a natural disaster. It was certainly a state of emergency.

I said, "What's next, God?" I took what little I had left from the house and put it into a storage unit until I knew where to go and what to do next. I was back at work within a few days, and my wife took our baby to her parents' house, which was a couple hours away. I stayed in a friend's tiny apartment on an air mattress as I talked to the bank, the government, the property managers, and anyone else who knew how to make sense of what had happened or what to do next.

Eventually, a plan was in order and navigated, a new house was secured, and I was able to get my family back under the same roof. When I opened the door to the storage unit to retrieve our belongings, the stench of the flooded home hit me. The items carried the same horrible smell, and the storage unit, which was one of the last remaining in the city due to demand, also happened to have a leaky roof. Boxes from the attic were soggy, and mold was growing on the remaining items. Anything we had salvaged was officially ruined. Pictures, critical documents, heirlooms, and clothes were destroyed.

That was how I learned not to ask God about what's next in such a condescending tone. You can't plan life; all you can do is be available for it. It's not a guided tour; it's not a journey. It's what your thoughts, actions, and decisions make it. That natural disaster may have been one of the best things to ever happen to me. Despite losing so many possessions, foreclosing on the house, dealing with the financial setbacks for many years, even with the timing of my daughter—especially with my daughter—it was the chance to start a new chapter and move on.

In the next few months, I received a promotion that moved us to Chicago. I was earning a six-figure salary in operations leadership with incentives in my twenties, which was a feat in itself in the middle of a recession and economic downturn. I had always wanted to live in Chicago, but I had only visited.

Life will hand you pickles, and you must learn how to relish them. Sometimes *not* getting what we want is a wonderful stroke of luck. I thought I wanted the nice home with the picket fence and all-American dog and family, but it wasn't the time or the place. I've learned that the problems I am going through many times are preparing me for what I'm really asking life for.

Moving to Chicago fulfilled everything I was missing. The building we moved into had almost the same number of residents as my hometown. I had always felt connected to all the people in the world, but Chicago was my official test. My new team was made up of analysts, statisticians, and specialists with Indian, African American, Polish, and South American heritage. I split my time in the upcoming years in that role and on the South side of Chicago, and I was a minority in both environments. Diverse and inclusive environments were giving me new perspectives every day, and I began to see the shortcomings and mentality that continue to hold much of Middle America back from the progress of the coasts.

At home, I was becoming more vocal with my wife. I started sticking up for myself in many situations. I began to mature and see and understand the patterns of behavior. I found an outlet in my health and dropped even more weight, likely a subconscious way of escaping, which is common in many crumbling relationships.

My wife saw the writing on the wall and discretely began to detach. She hired a personal trainer, dropped off our kid with a part-time nanny, and spent several months getting her body and mind in shape for a personal goal. She wanted to become Mrs. America and fulfill her long-lost goals. I supported it financially and encouraged her.

After spending our entire savings on lavish dresses, body-shaping and other beautification, she entered and won the state title. She went on to Las Vegas and competed in the Mrs. America contest, but she did not win. She convinced me that this platform would lead to more money, which would allow her to finally be able to contribute financially. Instead, she ended up spinning her newfound attention into the pursuit of a different life for herself.

Single fatherhood, with a junior executive role, in a large city where I had no family and limited friends proved to be an interesting challenge. Raising a toddler for several years alone, playing Mr. Mom, and trying to do the right thing was a double whammy that too many women and men do not get enough credit or resources for. However, the relief I felt from being out of that relationship somehow gave me the strength I needed to succeed. I took my daughter for her first haircut, picked her up and dropped her off at day care, took her for doctors' visits to solve constipation riddles, did potty-training, arranged playdates with other families, and tried to find balance for myself and her. Many people in that situation would have rushed into another relationship for relief, but I took it as an opportunity to find myself again. I needed to figure out what had gotten me into that situation and determine what behaviors I needed to avoid repeating to ensure history didn't repeat itself. It takes a village to raise a child, and I did it with no villagers, as so many others do.

For the next three years, I grew more in my understanding of life, self-love, and what our time on this big rotating rock is all about. Other problems grew tinier, and my focus narrowed to just taking care of myself and my daughter. I became emotionally intelligent, balanced, and structured, and I was also discovering my purpose. In a sense, I fell back in love with myself.

I had very few free moments, but when I did, I took advantage and used my time wisely by taking myself out to dinner and a movie, cycling on the lakefront, or reading a book by the pool. When you rush into another relationship, you're bound for a higher percentage of failure. However, when you take the time to become deeply self-aware, you learn not to settle. The person or people you choose to share your life with determine a lot about your future. They determine your mental health, peace of mind, happiness, finances, children's well-being, and so much more. Choose your relationships wisely.

Social media allowed me an outlet to share what was going on in my life, and people began to talk. I received several requests from single women to chat, made a brief appearance on an episode of my ex-wife's dating show to discuss her cheating ways, and found a way to inspire others through the power of story. That story helped lead me back to Iowa as a Chief People Officer with a growing private firm. A move that would shift the course of the next several years of my life, teach me about entrepreneurship, help me meet my current wife-who had to jump my trust issue hurdles, start a company of my own, and begin engaging with people and companies that needed a performance boost. My purpose is to make a difference in people's lives or add value to them. My vision is to create several companies or ways of doing this on a larger scale. I am not attempting to become the hero of my own story, but I want to help others relate to their lives.

We all have defining moments in our lives. Those were a couple of mine that helped me see my life and the world from a different perspective. Take a moment to chart out some of your defining moments in the next online activity. All lives have peaks and valleys—make sure to list both. Awareness comes from each.

CHAPTER 3

───ᴍ───

THE ART OF BALANCE

One of the biggest breakthroughs that most of my individual clients have reported back to me as positive growth has been in the form of balance improvement in their lives. Awareness is like the sun; when it shines on things, they are transformed. These are people who have an awareness of holistic wellness and are healthy professionals or entrepreneurs, but they're stuck. Many times, this is where we begin after our initial session.

From personal experiences and by taking them through exercises and conversations, I've learned that life balance is difficult. It's different for everyone, but the best way to keep your life in balance is to realize when it's not. Self-awareness is the best tool to discover this. In the same no-nonsense, practical, straightforward way, this tree of life tool is designed to show you how your life roots nourishing the environment they need will produce fruit for you. However, just like in nature, if not all of the roots are receiving the proper nutrients or care, the entire tree and its life are at risk. These are the energy blocks that I've seen in myself, that I also try to uncover with clients.

We are all born with the ingredients for a happy life, but most of us are still lacking the recipe. If I asked you to make me a cake and you just tossed eggs, sugar, flour, and butter in a bowl and handed it to me, I wouldn't eat it. They're not working together, you're probably missing certain amounts of the ingredients, and it's not likely to turn out well. I hope you understand the parallel I am attempting to draw. Many people are wandering through their lives out of balance, on autopilot, and it's not allowing them to even consider leading the happy, successful lives they are capable of. What's worse is that they don't know who to talk to about it without seeking paid or professional help.

This goes far beyond just work-life balance. It actually starts with your physical root, which influences your mental root, which can impact your occupational and social roots. If your physical root is not getting the proper love, which is an epidemic across the world right now due to our food and exercise choices, you will be struggling in other areas. In future chapters, we will look deeper into each of the roots to help you determine which ones aren't getting what they require to give you balance.

Many self-help books focus on one specific area of growth: physical, spiritual, leadership, career, or networking. In this book, we'll attempt to get under the surface from a holistic perspective to allow you an overall view into your life and the stories of others who are evolving through this every day. This will help you create a harmony of routines that are necessary to get unstuck or further evolve your level of awareness. While this chapter is called the "Art of Balance," there is actually some science we can apply here as well.

For instance, if you look at your overall wellness in the form of the four roots, begin to ponder what percentage each of them needs for you to feel at your personal best. It's likely not evenly distributed at 25 percent between the four roots. Each person has differing needs, and some individuals place heavier value or weight distribution in their current stage of life on certain roots. In order to go deeper, it will be helpful if you have understanding with each of them before we analyze them in more detail.

Your physical root is comprised of key health properties, like your weight, sleep, relaxation, illnesses or disease, sex life, and immune, nervous, and cardiovascular systems. Do you have the right physical activities? Are you stretching? Is your body free of stress? Our bodies, just like the trees, have interesting ways of telling us when things are not right. So many people avoid the early warning signs before realizing the damage is already done. Whether you're aware enough to understand the cause and effect of your physical root decisions is the larger question. This single root has the ability to affect your entire life here on planet earth, and there are many obstacles or mistruths in the way to take you off course.

Your mental root is directly influenced by the performance of your physical and vice versa. They share the same nutrients and resources. While most wellness experts put spiritual wellness in its own category, I liken it to your mental wellness. What are your beliefs about this life, your world outlook, and beyond? How is your emotional health or self-image? Have you healed from things in your childhood? Are you confident, growth-oriented, and spending time in positive environments and with positive people? What about your adult life? Are you emotionally intelligent and aware of yourself and others? Have you discovered your blind spots? Is someone there to surround you and help you with them? Are you thinking about your purpose or mission here on earth? Do you spend time praying, meditating, or contemplating the essence of the universe or creation? Would you say you are globally centric in your view of others and life itself? All of these things, and many more, make up your mental root system and could be areas to learn and grow with separately or on their own. There may be limiting beliefs that you were raised with that are also present or in the way to take you off course.

Occupational roots have a tendency to heavily influence the first two roots. We spend a lot of our waking hours in our jobs or careers, and if we are out of balance there, it's likely we're suffering elsewhere as a result. For this root, you need to specifically look at your workload, stress, career growth potential, job satisfaction, workplace drama, travel demands, wages, coworker relationships, and overall culture you surround yourself with. Many people spend more time with their coworkers or at their jobs than they do with their families, but we don't spend the same amount of time determining what we need or don't need in our lives through the gigs we align ourselves with. Some people work to live, and others have a mentality of living to work. This is the age-old adage that those who live to work have their lives centered on achievement in their profession, and it's a major source of meaning or satisfaction for them. Those who work to live have a different purpose. Jobs for them are only a means to get the funds necessary to fulfill other needs of their lives. Which side of the spectrum do you fall on? This is another important step in becoming more self-aware.

Last but not least is your social root. It is often neglected for the others and was mentioned in the "top five regrets of the dying" in an earlier chapter. What does your balance look like in time or experiences spent with friends, activities, traveling, or other support systems? Are you involved in your community? Do you have connections to groups, hobbies, or networking opportunities?

Many experts believe that addictions form from a lack of connections to life, and if they are not balanced, this root directly influences those on the bottom branches of the tree. Are you having fun? Do you have time built in for play—even as an adult—and do you create with others? Is there anyone you are mentoring? All of these things make up your social health, which is a key contributor to your overall balance in life. Maybe you even know someone who has so much social time built in that they are completely neglecting other important areas of their life.

Choosing where your energy goes is a mastery reserved for the self-aware. Ensuring you have an idea of what you need to thrive and then creating a routine to balance it all is easier said than done. If you go deep enough into reflection of the self, this balance will teach you what things matter to you and what things you can control.

Your energy should be spent living your best life for yourself and for others around you. Understanding what may sabotage you from living for the bigger things that matter is very important. Television, news, social media, drama, and consumerism take you away from creating. When you're not creating, you're just consuming. If you spend your days consuming, you're living the life others are wanting you to live for their benefit. This behavior creates regret at the end of this gift called life. I wish I had understood this at a much earlier age.

Many people live their entire lives without comprehending the bigger picture. Our purpose here on earth is to be in divine, unconditional love. We are all one, and oneness exists within the entire planet. Our modern-day lives distract us from living as nature intended, but there's an opportunity or a choice you can make to change it.

Fulfilling your purpose in this body will require you to have a balance to achieve it. True balance takes self-awareness.

We'll go deeper into limiting beliefs as we delve into each root. You'll begin to uncover the energy blocks or levels of awareness that you didn't realize existed within yourself. For now, I will leave you with a quote from George Orwell's *1984*, which was written in 1948 about a dystopian future that he imagined, which oddly enough has a familiar vision of our present:

> Heavy physical work, the care of home and children, petty quarrels with neighbors, films, football, beer and above all gambling filled up the horizon of the minds. To keep them (the people) in control was not difficult. All that

was required of them was a primitive patriotism which could be appealed to whenever it was necessary to make them accept longer working hours or shorter rations. And when they become discontented, as they sometimes did, their discontentment led nowhere, because being without general ideas, they could only focus it on petty specific grievances.

This novel explained a future when most of the world population had become victims of perpetual war, omnipresent government surveillance, and propaganda. Where are you putting your energy now? Why? Where should you be spending your time? The key to keeping your life balanced is to realize when it's not.

In the following activity on fixtheroots.com, take your time to create your root balance framework. What percentage of time in your best traditional weeks needs to be spent on each root? What are the nonnegotiable things that you need in order to feel balanced?

CHAPTER 4

PHYSICAL ROOT

I was sought out by a client who was fed up with his life and needed answers for his next steps. It was part career guidance, part life counseling, and part health coaching, but it started with a question: "Can you help me assess my situation?"

What started with one session turned into a multi-month deep dive into this business leader's root system. A solid six-figure career, climbing the I.T. world ladder, some startup investment, and experience had this lifelong learner and academic proud of his accomplishments, but he was concerned about his overall state of being. Having been a former rugby player and also in a semi-new marriage, his occupational root became so important and overwhelming that his physical appearance and health began to suffer. Add in some childhood limiting beliefs, and he was talking with counselors, therapists, and anyone else who could help him sort it out. When he was not getting what he needed from licensed practitioners, he sought additional help from me.

His main concerns were the amount of weight he had gained due to the stress, how his relationship was suffering due to work, his degrading confidence, and determining which career steps could help him balance it all. His food choices were not healthy, and exercise and sports were no longer a priority. Just making it through the workday was a challenge. This left very little time for anything more than a quick meal, a relaxing beverage, and sleep before repeating it all again the next day. It had been going on that way for years. I could relate—and maybe you can too.

When we broke down his root system, his needs, and his current balance, we found that he was spending 80 percent of his overall energy on his occupation. He was covering for team members, taking on new projects, and constantly monitoring the hardware and software environments. He was burned out. His ideal balance for the occupational roots was around

20 percent, and he realized his physical and social roots were suffering as a result, which was the sole reason for strain in his relationship. It seems practical to read about it, but this level of awareness is sometimes difficult when you're caught up in the moment. Getting perspective from others on the outside takes a fair amount of humility, and those who can get to this level of awareness have reached an important step. Many people will continue on until something goes horribly wrong because they are too afraid to address how they feel or be aware of what they are doing over the long term.

Considering that one in three American deaths is from heart disease and one in three is from cancer, you'd think that we'd have it figured out by now. That type of health scare from the body can create an awakening or shift for people to either change and survive or give up.

It takes an awareness of yourself, your thoughts, and your choices to avoid going down these paths. For me, it was easy to help my client because of my own story. I had been slightly obese due to my own poor choices, but I decided it was time for a change when I was trying to increase my life insurance policy.

After a health examination, I was declined the additional coverage due to several health factors, including my cholesterol, triglycerides, and blood pressure. I was blowing off steam with cheeseburgers and beer on the weekends and placing very little time on my physical wellness. At the time, it was more important to me that I spend my energy trying to get ahead financially because my relationship choices were draining my bank accounts and my time. Despite being athletic and health conscious, avoiding sweets, and having lean family members, I was on my way to heart disease or cancer via obesity. I could feel it, and I made a commitment to myself and my daughter that I would get my physical root the nutrients it needed to thrive because it would affect every other portion of my life. Looking back at old photos, I often wonder how bad my life was during those years to let myself grow to the size I had become.

I don't like to follow rules, I don't like anyone telling me what to do, and I definitely don't like fads or diets. Instead, I went with my own approach, which was based on my gut and intuition. I made a lifestyle change that I still maintain today: no supplements, no crazy workouts, and no programs that I needed to pay for or follow.

My weight loss from 240 pounds to 180 pounds came in the form of getting in touch with my body and leveraging science. As a result, my skin got clearer, I gained the mental clarity I needed, I sleep better, and I am a different person overall. I went back to nature and the root of the problems I was having. As a result, I maintain a primarily plant-based meal plan, void of complex carbs and refined sugars. I also decreased alcohol intake significantly, with the exception of a nice, red wine primarily. I don't touch processed foods, and I see what I ingest as a form of medicine with two outcomes. What I put in my body either fuels my energy and health or slowly depletes it. I have the choice to choose—even if I am on the run, have kids in tow, or am trying to save some money. With some fun workouts, pushing my body, and being generally overall in tune with it, the weight melted off in approximately seven months. I continue to fast for up to five days a few times a year to recenter myself or reset my immune system, and I still enjoy too many cheat meal pizzas with friends and family. It doesn't feel like work anymore to be healthier, and the cravings have almost completely subsided. I had to change my relationship with food and shift the energy elsewhere.

My client made a commitment to schedule workouts into his day, use it to energize his work, and get back into rugby. Decisions were made holistically to better balance every one of his nonnegotiable needs. It went well beyond physical wellness. At each appointment, he let me know what changes he had made since our last talk and how he was repurposing his energy. His relationship started to reap the rewards, and he got more results in a few months than he did in a few years via an approach that helped him get to the root of the problems.

His spouse joined in, and they began to communicate their needs to each other to get balance within their relationship. He had to have a conversation with his company executives about his time spent there. When that conversation didn't lean in his favor, he resigned to take time to focus on his future and next steps. I had not suggested that move, but it ultimately changed the trajectory of his life, which is very bright today. He fixed the roots, and as a result, he continues to enjoy the fruit.

Our stories are just small, semi-inspirational stories of people who figured it all out before it was too late. We didn't use medications, programs, or anything else; we simply had the awareness to recognize that things weren't optimal and found the courage and will power to make changes and fix them. A mind-set shift is needed across the world to further avoid the health crisis that has been occurring.

If you're wondering what I am talking about, please educate yourself with the World Health Organization data. In their most recent studies, here's what they've concluded:

- Globally, one in four adults is not active enough.
- More than 80 percent of the world's adolescent population is insufficiently physically active.
- Insufficient activity is one of the leading risk factors of death worldwide.
- Sufficient activity for adults 18–64 is considered 300 minutes of moderate exercise a week.

Now, here are the real, in-your-face, shocking realities and predictions of where we're headed:

- By 2025, as developing countries continue to grow, so will their amount of deathly diseases as a result of adopting Western lifestyles that include high-fat diets, smoking, and lack of exercise.
- Diabetes cases by 2025 will more than double from 1997 totals due to dietary and lifestyle factors.
- Cancer will remain one of the global leading causes of death by 2025, due to developing countries, and it will remain flat or decrease in industrialized nations like the United States due to awareness and the shift to more plant-based, health-, and environment-focused lifestyles.
- Annually, more than 15 million adults aged 20–64 are lost to premature and preventable deaths.

The reason I suggest that you work on your physical root first is that it's the most critical piece to you being here on earth, in this body, at this time. If you don't take care of that, you'll face many obstacles in trying to balance or get awareness in the rest of your life.

If you're not physically active today, start small and work toward the three hundred minutes of physical activity a week. Start with a couple of minutes for a couple of days per week. Thirty minutes is only 2 percent of your entire day, but you need to plan it to be successful. Don't wait for a health scare and a doctor to tell you to do it; by then, it may be too late.

Our bodies—if we are aware and listen to them—will tell us everything we need to know about how we are treating them. Our bodies are like the roots of the trees signaling their pain on the surface via bark, branches, and leaves. If you are not in a place to become physically active, try to get outdoors. When was the last time you got yourself into nature and took off your shoes? Studies have shown that putting your bare feet in grass, water, or sand has major health advantages.

Spending time in nature improves physical wellness, and it can tell you a great deal about your learning style and help you find your strengths. For many people, nature is a catalyst for self-awareness. For those with a strong physical root and awareness, movement is the biggest thrill in nature. When hiking a trail, the body understands and responds to the topography. For these kinesthetically adept, climbing rocks with all four limbs resonates, and peaking or summiting a mountain highlights the nature experience for them.

The socially strong love nature when it includes other people. Sharing stories around a campfire, group hikes, meeting others on the trail, and exchanging experiences are essential. People with strong interpersonal skills have a deeper connection when they can discuss the landscape or a wildlife sighting.

Those that have a strong mental root—or are developing the self—thrive with solo time in nature. Driven by strong intrapersonal intelligence, they find time to journal, reflect, and plan for the future. Solo nature experiences offer an opportunity to understand oneself, challenge boundaries, and learn to pace or meditate.

I take many getaways or vacations each year to reflect because I know my style and what I need. Interestingly enough, this book began with a dream I had about a forest, and it continued in my awakened state on a solo hiking trip in Colorado. A lot of the answers about life can be found in the silence of nature.

More advances in using nature to understand and improve physical wellness are coming. More natural-based solutions for learning, medicine, transportation, and industry in general are coming. Health data in upcoming decades will also make us even more aware of our bodies and overall longevity. When we can pair data with best practices, we can create measurable change—and what gets measured gets improved in most cases. What gets measured—and has your entire life depending on—it should improve exponentially.

Please take a moment to organize your physical root plan with the website resource labeled 'Physical Root Plan". You can categorize your needs into a weekly schedule. Making the time to prioritize this is key. It may take some tweaking and balancing, but physically aware people operate like this.

CHAPTER 5

MENTAL AWARENESS

Love is what we were born with. Fear is what we learned here.
—Marianne Williamson

D r. David R. Hawkins found a way to measure consciousness, and in poring over his work during the past few years, I found something profound that he revealed prior to his passing. Our collective consciousness as a planet and as a nation had been on a steady climb until the late 1980s, but then it started to decrease. By consciousness, I am specifically referring to the state or quality of awareness or of being aware of an external object or something within oneself. Our civilization went backward mentally.

In terms of spirituality, there are many paths to choose from to get to your ultimate truth. We all walk different paths, at different times in our lives, yet many of us, deep within our cores, believe in a shared truth—that there is a God or afterlife in the nonphysical realm and what we do in this lifetime will ultimately be judged. While there have been many earthbound examples, including Jesus, Buddha, Muhammed, and Mother Teresa, who have achieved enlightenment on earth, a majority of the human race has failed to achieve the results that are possible. Hence the regrets that become so known on our deathbeds. These individuals or deities did not measure success by how much money they earned—but by how many lives they positively impacted. Imagine if that were the new definition of the term *millionaire*? I did not make one million dollars, but I inspired more than one million people in my time here on earth. That is the new level of mental awareness that it will take to shift into the upgraded energy completely as a planet.

What holds us back from living our lives this way or more in the present? It is very simply put: fear. Lao Tzu stated, "If you are depressed, you are living in the past. If you are anxious, you are living in the future. If you are at peace, you are living in the present." These thoughts and feelings of suffering are based in fear. This is the type of understanding of self that makes up the mental root. Many people who have achieved success and lost it did not have a well-maintained mental root. It primarily suffers from our childhood, our surroundings, our exposure to certain situations, and our beliefs or experiences passed down from others.

Evidence from the World Health Organization suggests that more than 50 percent of the world's population is affected by mental illness with an impact on self-esteem, relationships, and ability to function in everyday life. Your mental root can affect your physical root as well, leading to further problems in being able to live a happy, functioning, fulfilled life.

If you look at your tree of life assessment results and see where you assessed, you'll see where you currently are in your life awareness and how much possibility and potential you have to continue climbing. Those who treat their mental and spiritual fitness as seriously as they treat their physical fitness are climbing their way up to joy from branch to branch.

How do you move forward with this great information? I will be the first to say that I've devoted much of my adult life to self-development. Learning, teaching, advising, testing, reading, and practicing take time. Self-development does not happen overnight; it takes more than one source, and while I'd love it to be my books or tools, it will likely have to come from a variety of sources that are referred to you or that you seek out. There's no silver bullet solution, but just by taking the assessment and reading this chapter, you're ahead of the pack. So, what's stopping you from achieving holistic balance, success, health, or happiness? If every day is a gift and that's why we call it the 'present', then why aren't you treating it like a gift? Let's get to the root of your energy blocks to answer that question.

Please take a minute to circle the following beliefs that you still hold in your awareness—even at the smallest levels:

1. I'm not somebody who follows through.
2. I'm good at starting projects, but I can't finish them.
3. I'm not an expert.
4. Nobody cares about what I have to say.
5. I'm not perfect. Why would anybody listen to/buy from/hire me?

6. I didn't work hard enough on this.
7. I'm not worth it.
8. I don't deserve [money, recognition, success].
9. I don't have time.
10. My family isn't entrepreneurial. ("Smiths don't start businesses!")
11. People will judge me—or my family will shun me.
12. I'm a creative.
13. I'm *not* creative.
14. I'm a procrastinator.
15. I'll sound stupid.
16. Somebody has thought of this before.
17. Other people can do it better than I can.
18. Nobody is interested in my ideas.
19. My idea is weird. It's not the norm.
20. If I succeed, I won't be able to sustain it.
21. I don't have the skills.
22. I'll never be creative/analytical/mathematical/good enough at selling enough to be an entrepreneur.
23. People who have something to sell are evil.
24. Nobody would want what I have to offer.
25. I don't know enough.
26. I'm not a [numbers, business] person.
27. The people who are successful in this are out of your league.
28. You're not going to be successful—so there's no point in trying.
29. I'm too old.
30. I'm too young.
31. I owe it to others to always work *for* them.
32. I'm beneath these people.
33. I'm a quitter. I don't finish things. I don't persist.
34. I'm lazy.
35. Entrepreneurs are sleazy.
36. I'm not original enough.
37. People like me don't (inspire others, follow their dreams, become successful).
38. People won't take me seriously because I'm (female, male, young, old, fat, thin).

39. I'll look foolish.
40. I don't feel like I could give enough value.
41. I've tried it before and failed, so I'll fail if I try again.
42. I can't because I have kids. I can't because I …
43. Regardless of how hard I might work at something or how well I might do, I'll never measure up.
44. I will always avoid pursuing goals that matter to me.
45. What is meant to be will happen; it is what it is.
46. I can't ask for anything. I'll be rejected.
47. I don't/wouldn't know where to start.
48. The only way to success is to go to college, get a degree, and work your way up the corporate ladder.
49. I don't have the willpower.
50. I'm just not motivated.
51. I'm happy with how things are now.
52. I'm not smart enough.
53. I can't do that.
54. There is no point.
55. I don't have enough money.
56. I don't have enough support.
57. I don't have the connections.
58. I'm too shy.
59. I'm too scared.
60. That's just not "me."
61. I'm not tech savvy.
62. I don't know what I want.
63. Now is not the time; my country is behind.

After leaving Corporate America's large, hierarchy-based organizations, I realized how many blocks I had. While I had overcome my fears of public speaking to large audiences, to pitching, and to facilitating major business decisions and consulting executives, I still had my own blocks. By working with entrepreneurs almost exclusively for two years, I realized how I was holding myself back from evolving in my occupational root—and all others.

I used to get nervous speaking to anyone in an executive-level, C-suite role. When I got to know a few, I realized they were no different than I was in many cases. In some instances, I had a wider range of experience and leadership due to my roles in big business. While they had small enterprises consisting of a couple hundred people and were growing, I was used to leading operations for thousands and managing P/L of organizations many times that size. Once I started to understand and break through my limiting beliefs, my mental root and confidence improved. Following that, I felt a strong emotional intelligence and a notable wisdom, well beyond my age, I've been told. I was learning about my own self-awareness, myself, and my blocks, and I was creating a path forward.

What's holding you back? What's getting in your way? What are your blind spots or opportunities? If you're not asking yourself these questions all the time, then you're not truly going deep enough to improve your mental fitness. Who hurt you? Why do you fear so much?

Asking these questions of yourself and getting feedback from others is a very important step in getting under the surface to determine the health of your mental root. Self-awareness is far from a soft skill, and it can be one of the biggest predictors of success in life, but you need to heal.

Combining these answers with actionable learning and development is critical to your happiness while you're on this big, spinning, round rock in the sky. When people ask me how I'm doing, I usually say, "I'm just trying to be the best me I can be. How are you?" It's the truth, and it often engages others to open up, humbly.

As humans, we often forget that we're just as much a part of nature as our plant, animal, and earth counterparts. When we get in tune with it, we can see the similarities for how we could be living our best lives. For example, trees throughout the seasons advance and evolve each year just like we do. Let's compare them to our New Year's resolutions. We plan out our year in January and start exerting a lot of energy toward goals and improvement. By spring, we begin to see some fruits of our labors. Our leaves and life begin to grow and develop. In summer, we thrive and continue our trek toward success. In fall, our leaves begin to discolor and fade, while we try to make one last push toward our accomplishments. By winter, all of our efforts for the year have come and gone, faded as we begin to think about how we will continue our growth again in the following year. The same applies to business. While time is nonlinear in the long run, this linear thinking of humans is right on pace with how the rest of life around us tends to work.

For anyone who watches or studies birds or specific animal behaviors, you've likely noticed that they operate like some of our most successful humans: awake early, slightly before or with the sun as it rises, a light meal if they are lucky, and off to work on building nests, finding food, or other activities. By early afternoon, they're playing with others or taking a brief moment to rest. Maybe they are even singing or having a little fun in the sun. As the sun begins to fade, it's one final meal and a chat with their friends and/or family and quiet time. If you think about yourself as a small child, it's likely very similar behavior.

If you can attempt to remember what you were like and what drove or motivated you as a child—before the fear-based world got a hold of you—then you should take every opportunity to do just that. Many people discover their purpose by thinking back to childhood and becoming aware of what happened to them and how it affected them—and then helping others solve the same problems. They find the things they realize they've always wanted to do, and they go for it.

Why are you not passionately pursuing what sets your soul on fire? It's likely that you haven't taken the time to ponder it or are afraid to move forward. For me, it was both. Some limiting beliefs had me thinking very small. When I set my vision on the end of my life and all of my goals to be long term, I realized I could go about them in many different ways.

We often overestimate what we can do in a year, but we underestimate what we can do in ten years. After all, I am going to continually grow and lose my leaves every year, but what really matters is that I continue to keep my roots healthy, grow upward, and then, under the surface, keep supporting other trees in my network and family. While we have made great progress in science and quantum physics, we're still not able to confirm many of these connections, how dark matter works, how we're connected to consciousness, facts regarding the unconditional love we feel following departure from our bodies, and many other important questions that could affect our mental roots. However, what an exciting time to be alive and learn or teach along the way!

"Beginning with the end in mind" is a famous business adage from Stephen Covey, and I have one particular client who was going through a very important transition in her life as well. She was a mother and a professional, somewhat successful, but she had been caught up in all of the things that come at us in today's modern world. In her thirties, she was diagnosed with diabetes and was not living up to her potential. She was stuck on autopilot in her life and felt completely out of balance. She didn't see a solution forward. What had once been reading, exercise, yoga, and other activities to fill free time was now completely different. Social media, food shows, full series of television via streaming services—not to mention shopping to keep up with all of the "things" that she saw others having—were the new comforts and self-therapies. She had not identified her purpose, did not do anything constructive with her free time, and was basically just trying to get through each day. In the everyday stress of a busy professional, she turned to mind-numbing comfort as her pleasures.

Don't get me wrong, I enjoy a good sandwich, TV show, and buying something new. However, over the years, I've learned that they are not the important things or activities I want to spend a majority of my free time doing. Most sports and television are no longer comforts for me in stressful times; in fact, in many cases, they create the stress. No one is going to remember that I watched all twelve seasons of a television show at the end of my life, but people *will* remember that I cut it all out to write a book with hopes of waking up people all over of the world.

If we're not careful, media, advertisements, and greed can overwhelm us and start making decisions for us. My client began to understand that by going through her root balance exercise, having discussions, and committing to change. Soon enough, she had organized yoga, meditation, and reading spaces in her home for herself again. She reenrolled at the gym and had her husband in awe of the changes she was making. He became inspired and began to make some changes of his own. They talked about their balance, and they carved out some time individually for balanced needs, deeper thinking, date nights, and planning. Kid number two was on its way the last time I checked in, and holistically, the family was doing much better. No more diabetes, healthy lifestyles, time together spent on experiences with each other—and not stuff or sitting on the couch all evening or weekend.

We are all souls who are taking part in a physical experience on this planet. Our bodies are simply vehicles made up of many different components that help us achieve what we've agreed to come here to do. When we begin to think and act like nature intended and ignore or eliminate the negative energy distractions around us, the process begins to unfold. Like the tree, sometimes you need others to help identify the pests or diseases. Get under the surface to remove them in an effort to continue your holistic health. Minimalism is a very important thing in many people's lives. If you're not familiar with it, it is time to research how the amount of choices in front of you could be distracting you from living the life you were truly meant to live.

Take some time to reflect on the limiting beliefs you circled that may be holding you back. Where did they come from? Are they true? Answer the purpose questions on the website to help you become more aware of your overall reason for being and your end-of-life wishes. Dreams plus goals plus action are part of the winning formula. Don't let it fade or become unimportant.

CHAPTER 6

~~~m~~~

SOCIAL AWARENESS

If you're so focused on your mental, physical, and occupational needs, as many of us are, you're going to be more prone to an utter and complete breakdown. Having social balance in your life, regardless of age, is extremely important. This is not just about time for family and friends; it is also about getting involved in activities, your community, and mentoring others. Make time for fun activities, experiences, travel, hobbies, or connecting with others. Successful people find a way to integrate these things into their work. Some studies show the importance of "play" in nature and with humans, and I cannot overstate how crucial it is in balancing all of your roots. At the same time, too much focus on this root, done inappropriately, can also unbalance you.

A newly retired Teacher had recently lost her husband earlier than planned via illness and became stuck in her life. She was grieving through this time and trying to handle everything with the estate on her own. There were many things to figure out, and she was attempting to heal at the same time. Many people never quite move on from an event like this, but she had a lot of life left and was very balanced everywhere else in her life. Physically, she may have been one of the most fit sixty-five-year-old women I've ever met. Her mother is nearing one hundred years old, and I firmly believe that this client will live well past that age with advancements in technology and medicine to compliment her healthy lifestyle. Mentally, she has always been balanced, but she decided to take up a meditation practice and explore new methods of spirituality that she had not considered before.

Occupationally, she was very busy substitute teaching as needed, helping with her grandchildren, and enjoying the life of a retired schoolteacher of thirty-five years. However, she had no social balance, and it was beginning to impact her and others around her. Quite frankly, she was lonely and not interested in joining support groups, putting herself out there to meet new people, or finding group social activities to fill her time.

Social aspects often make up a big piece of the day in retirement, yet she could not figure out why she was so negative for most of her days. She would find one or two things to complain about and then repeatedly barrage her family with these complaints about life and how it was not fair. Much of it was part of the healing process after losing a spouse, but it was very much spurred on by not having the awareness that this was the missing root that needed some love.

We had her take the assessments to discover what kind of balance she needed and see where she was spending her time to identify the gap. She was also an early tester of the tree of Life Assessment, helping me validate the results.

This retiree is actually my mother-in-law, and while she is not really a client, we have had hundreds of deeper discussions about life, love, and awareness. I'm pleased to report that she has also gotten 100 percent balanced with her time over the past several months and years. As the healing set in, we set her up with an online dating profile to meet people. She now goes on occasional dates, has friends all over the city, is involved in wine-tasting classes, gets invited to neighborhood gatherings, walks the trails with friends, and is now sometimes too busy to help us with the grandchildren.

We love seeing her continue on with the next chapter of her story, and we also join her on some of her travels, which she books each winter and spring. For someone who did not place a lot of importance on her social root throughout her life, she is now completely aware of its importance on her overall attitude and life. She regrets not taking part in many of the experience-building times or trips with her late husband, and she encourages her daughter to pack up and travel along as she is able.

Being able to cultivate real social wellness is something that seems to be getting harder and harder for each generation. We've been so busy and consumed in many cultures that it can be difficult to find the time to connect authentically with others and build lasting, deep relationships at work, in the community, and around the planet. You'd think that the internet and social media would be the perfect tools for this, but in most cases, they are not. Effective love for your social root involves having great communication skills, meaningful relationships, respect of yourself and others, and creating a support system for yourself. We used to do it with local tribes in ancient times, but the way we currently view tribes has changed significantly.

You are the average of the five people you spend the most time, and that phrase hits close to home. When I look back on life and the many different groups of friends I surrounded myself with, I can see the truth in this. While it was great to have a core group of friends who remained close from childhood, our spouses were quick to see that many of us had been stuck in a time warp. As hard as it's been, I had to begin to distance myself from them. We were repeating the same rituals, the same views of life, the same judgments, and the same competitions we were raised with. While some of us were able to get out of the box on occasion, we ultimately did not take large chances or risks for fear of judgment or failure from friends and others.

When you start to surround yourself with others who are aligned with your way of thinking—and with similar hopes, goals, visions of life, and interests, you begin to wake up to what is possible. No matter how difficult it is, you may need to branch off from family or friends who no longer share your same longing for living a fulfilled life. There are two quotes that come to my mind from wise individuals that perfectly sum up social wellness in my life. I live by them—and maybe they can speak to you too:

> Great minds discuss ideas. Average minds discuss
> events. Small minds discuss people.
> —Eleanor Roosevelt

> Show me your friends, and I'll show you your future.
> —John Wooden

You can't soar like an eagle if you're flying with turkeys. Go to the website, locate the 'My Five Birds' page and capture the five people you spend the most time with outside of your coworkers and family. If you don't have five people you interact with outside of this, there's your first mission. If you've got a list of three to five people, ask yourself if how they lead their life is more like a brave, soaring eagle or a turkey.

Now, if you're stuck and don't know where you'd like to be or go, make a new list of people or eagles you already know who you look up to or admire. You can include those who are doing things you'd like to be doing. Make that your new list. Striking a friendship or mentorship can be easy when we tell another person we admire them and want to surround ourselves more with their presence.

CHAPTER 7

~~~m~~~

CLIMBING THE TREE

T hings are often deeper than they seem. Once you've stopped searching among the branches for your truth and get to the root of the problems, things will change for you. After overcoming some difficult obstacles, you should eventually get to a place of self-love. This is when everything changes for people. Their entire outlook, habits, and behaviors change. They start ascending to a higher awareness of life and what it means. They are waking up or becoming woke, as it's sometimes referred to, which requires letting go.

Many times, people don't even realize they're blocking their own blessings by holding onto things or the past. Healing, changing, growing, and getting back to a positive energy are required to ascend toward the enlightened days ahead. It's found by following your heart instead of the crowd and choosing knowledge and awareness over the smoke and mirrors of ignorance. In many cases, rising above the norms requires a rule-breaking mentality.

Once you've understood yourself and learned to love yourself, your journey through complete transformation on your way to mastery begins. This type of transition takes consistency, routine, and commitment to pour everything you have into a higher purpose. If you feel you've already understood life and your purpose for being here, you're on the right path. If you've got a pulse, you've got a purpose.

When you come to this understanding, you will have to find times to clear your mind, go silent, let go of control, listen to your intuition, and trust, which can be easier said than done. However, once you've mastered it, you will find that you become like a human highlighter when you enter a situation or a room. You brighten everything you come into contact with. These are the people who are inspiring others through their expression for life. They are often thinking large, have more global viewpoints, and can relate or show empathy in just about any situation. They naturally want to help others—despite whatever large endeavors they already have going on. Their character, personality, and wisdom will often be cherished by those who know or come into contact with them. They are complete joy in their daily dealings with life. They have understood that the purpose of life is having a life of purpose. They pursue it daily.

As they continue to practice self-mastery and develop into the most blissful, complete version of themselves, the teaching occurs for others. They've been through the pain, they overcame whatever adversity has come their way to this point of their life, and they've come to understand unconditional love for the earth and everything that is a part of it. They are an example for others to follow, regardless of which religion they practice. They help transform others. Do you know anyone like this or anyone who has reached this stage of life?

So how do you know if you're ascending past traditional planes of self-awareness? There's a lot of speculation and theory about specific symptoms that you may experience as you're coming over to the light, as I like to say. While there are numerous resources available to research on your own, I will share my experiences and my wife's experiences on our journey. My ascension happened approximately three years before hers, and I kept notes, discussed it with others who had been through it, and completely immersed myself in it. Things felt and seemed so different, but I couldn't put a name to what was occurring. When I saw my wife going through the same exact transformation three years later, I knew I had to document this unfolding for others who were looking for guidance during that time. While I do not believe these happen for everyone, I believe it's the body's way of helping us through the process. It is different for each person, depending on what they need to change.

STRONG EMOTIONS

As a male who previously shed tears approximately once every ten or fifteen years since childhood, I could not figure out how I was becoming so soft and sensitive. I grew up in an all-female household after age nine, and I currently live in a house with my family of four females. I naturally felt like I had a good balance for my masculinity as a result of my environment. The rapid change in emotions that washed over me in the year of my ascension was nothing to joke about. There were two specific points that moved me to tears in front of my wife, and they came completely out of nowhere. The first was some healing that I didn't realize I needed from my childhood. I found myself sobbing uncontrollably in our living room over some last remaining anger I had to part ways with. It came during a random conversation and ended with me having snot bubbles coming from my nose, deep wheezing, loud sniffles and snorts, and tears like I had never experienced in my life. While I was embarrassed in the moment, the relief I felt after having someone hear what I had been holding in my subconscious for decades was immeasurable. It set the stage and opened the door for the rest of my ascension. I got the ugly cry out of the way.

The second point of strong emotion came in an unpredicted moment of joy and bliss. While having dinner in the Caribbean for our anniversary, I absolutely lost it in the restaurant. I was overwhelmed to the point of tears by the beauty of life, the sunset, the environment, and the love for her, for life, and for the journey. I heard whispers, congratulations, and some advice right in the moment from people who were already passed as we waited for our food. Maybe it was all in my mind, but likely not. Thank goodness our table faced a mountain range, and I had my back to all other guests. Otherwise, they'd likely wonder why this grown man was sobbing through his dinner.

For my wife, her strong emotions came in the form of extreme gratitude one summer. Throughout our relationship, I had never seen her so alive and in such deep thought. It was like the brightest light bulb remained above her head every day for three months straight. She kept ordering more books and journals and listening to more podcasts on self-development— when she previously had enjoyed a good murder-mystery. We discussed symptoms, how she was going through what I had gone through, and how we were happy to be on the journey together. We knew we could help one another through the process—and we knew how far we wanted to go in helping others who were feeling the same feelings.

CHANGES IN SLEEP

Needing more or less sleep than normal is a commonly reported symptom of this process. As you're letting go of the past energies, or you're healing, a lot of change is occurring as you sleep. I specifically had vivid dreams, woke up most mornings around three o'clock, and found myself constantly asking questions, listening, and praying for the world I was hoping to create. As a result, I was tired during the daytime and needed to protect my energy much more than before during the daytime.

My wife started waking up at four forty-five every morning. A workout, being at peace with herself to begin her day, and easing into each day came with the amount of stillness she gained during her ascension. She still maintains the same schedule today. Her physical root is the most important to her, and I like to say that my mental root is my top priority. While she is working out, I am usually enjoying my second sleep of the morning or simply easing into my day with meditation, reading, or organizing the details of my day.

RELATIONSHIP CHANGES

It can be very hard to let go of family relationships and friendships, but it often happens during the process. Your circle becomes smaller, and it usually includes others who match your same levels of awareness. You might realize that some friendships or family members were never meant to be in your life and may be holding you back. Your relationship might become a personal problem for you once you've ascended. Removing negative energy or influence from your daily life becomes immediately more important to you than ever before.

As you're planning social activities, you may start to ask yourself questions or second guess the people or events. What will the energy of this event be like? Is that friendship rooted in unconditional love and not judgment? How far has this family member come in evaluating their own awareness—and how do I feel when I am with them?

As my wife ascended, we found ourselves at a birthday party for a mutual friend. She brought her best friend, and we traveled out of state for the weekend to connect and celebrate with others.

After one day around the group, which we traditionally saw every year around that time, we looked at each other and had to huddle up. "Let's leave right away in the morning ... before the others wake up. Not to be rude, but simply to get back to the light—and away from the darkness that we now see is running these friends' lives." The darkness was referring to the group's mentality in terms of what was important and the fear or disappointment of life. Those successful people are still acquaintances, but they are not on the same page with this gift called life. My wife lost a best friend that weekend. It was not by any instance or event or mistake; it was simply a realization via ascension.

LACK OF APPETITE

My body was simply resetting and learning how to not rely on food all the time. It was a test of willpower and mentality with a side bonus of resetting my immune system. Periods of extended fasting became extremely important to me for some reason. I had not fasted before—it was not a part of religion for me to not eat for six or seven days at a time—but I felt like it had to be done.

I did not know anyone else who was doing it, but I researched the proper ways of doing it and the risks and benefits, and I really enjoyed it after the second day. The first two days of not eating brought me headaches, irritability, and low energy, but it was the exact opposite for the remainder of the fast. When I felt like I was going to break, I would slowly reintroduce simple-to-process foods and lemon water. I would not recommend doing this without the supervision of a physician, but I can say that my lack of appetite and desire to fast was highest during my ascension. Fasting is not only intermittent. Some individuals report an increased appetite during this process.

HEIGHTENED SENSITIVITIES

Loud noises, loud people, bright lights, technology, and anything too noisy or bold may start to bother you more than before. Maybe it's simply the body or soul's way of having you detox from certain things. If you've ever had a friend who seemed a bit eccentric or loud, get ready for how loud they're going to seem in your presence now. Have a child who is sometimes loud? Get ready for decibel levels that you cannot believe you haven't noticed before. Taking more time away from your phone or computer to get into nature or do something quiet will be a natural inclination.

As they ramp up their awareness, some people report nausea, aches and pains, memory loss, night sweats, anxiety, feelings of stress, and other body ailments. These common side effects can be created by numerous conditions; ideally, the big five will help you understand the change you're going through or preparing to go through. You cannot force yourself into it. Everyone ascends at a different time in life, and many people never do. I am not aware of any scientific or medical studies that explain this. When spirituality, consciousness and science converge with each other someday, maybe we'll be able to understand the process better. For now, we must rely on each other's experiences and books like this and others to guide us.

CHAPTER 8

ATTENTION WAR

As mental, physical and awareness levels in industrialized nations go backward, predictions note that less industrialized nations will follow the same trends in years to come. Not all nations will experience it, however, and several countries are aware and have put practices in place to help their economies move forward, keep their citizens living longer, spread wealth throughout—versus limiting it to the top 1 percent—and protect their part of the earth from dangerous levels of manmade disruption.

So what changed so dramatically in the 1980s that caused consciousness to start declining? What caused these unprecedented death rates and the downward spiral that prevented us from moving forward as humans? There is not one specific answer, but it has a lot to do with marketing, its accessibility, and how it evolved as the industrial age transitioned to the information age. Television and internet availability in households increased, meaning more advertising access in the eighties and nineties into today. Smartphone penetration levels increasing across our globe and now our phones & TV's compete for more of our attention, which means it is literally controlling much of the population's thoughts, behaviors, and actions. Advertisers have found a way to utilize our conscious levels, emotions, and fears to sell us certain products and services that continue to move us backward as a civilization—all for profit.

Some people claim the commercials and advertisements don't work on them. Subconsciously, you might not even be aware of how your life has been impacted by them. Let's take your smartphone as an example. It's like a lifeline. In today's world, many people feel anxious when they're without it for more than a few minutes. It started as a comfort, in case of emergency, but now it wakes us up, it tells us where to go and how to get there, and it helps us communicate throughout the day. If we let it, it can take control of our attention for most of our waking lives.

Social media engineering has caused people to become addicted to the dopamine hits they get with its repeated notifications. The devices and applications are all competing for your attention—and your children's attention—and, for the most part, they don't care how it impacts your life. As long as the advertising dollars come in from all of the information leveraged, they are happy. It has singlehandedly changed how we learn, altered the neural pathways of our brains, and prevented us from concentrating on things for long periods of time due to the distractions that it drives.

Items you didn't even realize you needed to purchase magically appear via sponsored advertisements. It's even done by demographics and classes of mental states. Is it any wonder that the NFL, beer, gambling, low-energy music, and UFC fans all seem to be in the same crowd? Where on the tree of life do many of them likely sit—and what else could you market to them based on their views of life? As you become aware of the impact marketing has on entire crowds of people, your eyes will begin to see things differently in your own life.

A recent trip to Las Vegas to speak at a conference included a lot of watching and learning about human behavior. I used to love Las Vegas, but it is predictable at best once you've reached a certain awareness level.

CHAPTER 9

BREAKING THROUGH

O nce you get clear on a purpose and dedicate all of your energy, vibration, and frequency of effort toward something—with limited distraction or mental fog—your breakthrough to the surface and your personal growth will be exponential. It is a force of nature, like a tree. You may not see it in terms of above ground success, but deep below, your roots have been established and are ready. This does not happen at the same time for everyone. The day you plant the seed is not the day you eat the fruit. Ascending to life breakthroughs only happens after deep internal transformation. It can take what seems like a lifetime, and everyone has a different growth plan and timing. Many will never break through or thrive, but we are all given the opportunity and sometimes it takes 10 years to get to the 1 year that changes everything.

There are countless stories of individuals who have had to overcome something before reaching success. Two of my favorite stories that resonate with me are Colonel Harland Sanders and J. K. Rowling. Both stories feature uncanny timing and are relatable.

Colonel Harland Sanders, an American businessman, was best known for founding the Kentucky Fried Chicken restaurant chains. While he passed away in 1980, his name and image still adorn the franchises. Many people have not heard the backstory to his success. There are many variations of his story, but most include a lot of inaccuracies. His autobiography tells the real story of a lost individual who spent time working as a farmer, a streetcar conductor, a soldier, a fireman, an insurance salesman, a steamboat operator, and a secretary among many other odd jobs. Whether he failed at those or got bored is up for debate, but one thing is not. He enjoyed cooking fried chicken and learned it at a young age due to leaving his home at age thirteen. However, it wasn't until he was sixty-two that he franchised his secret recipe and began to sell it to other restaurants. Reportedly using his last hundred dollars of retirement savings from social security, following many trials and tribulations in life, he traveled the United States looking for purchasers of the recipe. He went into their restaurants, brought his secret seasoning and recipe, showed them how to cook it, had them taste it, and then made an offer for sharing revenue. This evolved into the brick-and-mortar restaurants we see across the globe. By the time he passed at the age of ninety, there were an estimated six thousand outlets in forty-eight countries. Life happened through him—but not until nearly the end of his life of struggle and after being nearly broke and desperate.

Joanne Rowling—better known by her pen name J. K. Rowling—is the author of the Harry Potter fantasy series of books and films. She has a similar story. She had to go through poverty, the death of her mother, a divorce, odd jobs, and more before taking a chance on her writing. Growing up with an estranged father and a mother who had multiple sclerosis was just the beginning. She also endured a failed marriage, being jobless, being broke, and taking care of a child on her own. She had the courage to admit she was on welfare, was clinically depressed, and was contemplating suicide right before taking a chance on writing an idea that had been on her mind for years. The award-winning British author, film producer, screenwriter, and philanthropist has set records for book sales and donated sizable portions of her earnings to research for multiple sclerosis, anti-poverty, and children's welfare nonprofits.

While hindsight is always clearest, imagine if these two global icons had been focused on these efforts in early adulthood. While neither would likely have been able to produce the same output without the journey, it's a matter of perspective. If the purpose of life is to have a life of purpose, then why don't we learn about this early in life? We gain self-awareness via indirect feedback or learning, but self-development and finding purpose are not formally taught. School doesn't teach it directly, and workplaces rarely do. We chase many things all at once until we finally get to the moment where it all makes sense. The jobs, the projects, and the ideas sometimes teach you a little bit about your ultimate destination.

There's a Chinese proverb that states it well: "If you chase two rabbits, both will escape." If you put your efforts in multiple purposes, ideas, or jobs early on, you won't capture any success. We should be guided to these things with a clearly defined purpose that is established when we're younger. It should be based on our strengths, energies, intuition, and what excites us. It should help others, it should make you a livable wage, and it should be grounded in what the world needs. It should not be determined by your parents or others. If you can blend your personal interests and joy with your occupation, then you're on the right track. Since an estimated 80 percent of the American workforce will be contracted by the year 2030 (Source: Accenture Tech Vision), there is a chance for many future generations to receive help in building their dream jobs or companies.

Multiple goals can be difficult to meet. Singular defined goals, where you are not easily distracted, create a purpose. We're taught to think of goals in a calendar year or sometimes in three to five years if we're really focused, but many people are changing this approach by setting end goals for their lives based on *purpose.*

There is a very stark contrast between *end goals* and *means goals.* Think of it as a means to an end. There may be different ways to get to a goal (means), but at the conclusion, you either succeed (end) or fail. Instead of saying that you want to grow your insurance company by 5 percent in the next fiscal year, what if you simply said you wanted to build a legacy company to hand off to your children, support your community, and make a difference in people's lives along the way?

I am not discounting the importance of annual goals and business strategies, but by getting very clear and starting with the end in mind, you find flexibility to achieve your goals by any means necessary. Layer in the tactics and plan to get there via whatever cycle you deem appropriate. Startups have begun to pitch their business ideas by saying, "Here's the problem, here's why it's important to people, and here's my unique ability that puts me in position to solve it."

Putting all your energies and focus into one overarching problem or series of problems is a recipe for success. Whether it's developing a way to make chicken crispier and tastier or helping people dream again, it's up to you. Mark Twain said, "The two most important days of your life are the day you were born and the day you find out why." If you can develop the self-awareness that is necessary to find out why and align all of your efforts toward it, you will have accomplished the greatest goal.

Go to the website and fill out your purpose statement. Unless you've already determined yours, this should not be an easy task. Keep it simple and to the point. It should not be more than three sentences. If done correctly, this statement and vision should guide your decisions moving forward. It's who you believe you are to your core and what you're here for.

Contact us if you'd like to discuss it with a mentor.

CHAPTER 10

─────∽៣∼─────

HARVESTING YOUR FRUIT

Once you've gotten close to the top of the tree of life, it's time to pick your rewards. The final thing to grow on a fruit tree is the actual fruit. If you've stayed diligent in nurturing it, the things you've worked for will eventually grow or happen. Until then, it's important to see life as a tree likely does. You'll need to remember your roots, stand tall and proud regardless of the climate or circumstances, go out on a limb on occasion, be content with your surroundings and enjoy the view as you grow. Most important, is to trust that the growth is coming, even if silent or slow. One does not dig up a plant or tree to see if the growth is happening.

When all the conditions align, you'll know it and feel it in your heart. You will feel an intense desire to break out of any restrictive or life-draining situations. You'll have found yourself and your purpose and will be directing all of your decisions toward it whenever possible. You'll want to remove yourself from things or people that no longer serve you or your mission.

You will feel overwhelming bursts of creativity and be inspired at a very high rate. It could be images, music, art, nature, or anything else that motivates you. You'll have a deeper yearning for spiritual connections and revelations. Everything will feel new or altered as you find your way on your new path. Teachers will start to come out of the woodwork to help you. Motivating videos, books, events, and people will come into your life. Life is happening through you and for you—and for other people. Your new track will speak to you at profound levels and make you feel differently as you walk on your new path. Others will notice too.

Messages will start to appear for you. It may happen in random ways, and it will be up to you to attempt to understand what they mean. Once you are more in tune with harmony, the seasons, and the natural cycles of the earth, your understanding of self and even business will improve.

Improving your emotional, mental, physical, and spiritual balance will make you stronger, clearer, and more aligned with your best self. You'll likely even view animals and plants differently on the rest of your journey. You will feel a sense of connectivity to all and a direct experience of being whole.

You will feel unconditional love for all life—and in all forms. Many people believe that we are here on earth to get to this state of awareness. Until now, there has not been a road map or care plan for this growth journey. Thanks for seeking it out with me and for helping build it for many moons and for many others to come.

To recap your work, you should have completed the following self-awareness exercises via www.fixtheroots.com to truly do the deep work that is necessary to grow and develop:

1. Complete the tree of life assessment.
2. Chart your defining moments journey line.
3. Identify your root balance framework.
4. Document your weekly physical root plan.
5. Circle your limiting beliefs and answer your purpose questions.
6. Complete your five birds survey.
7. Complete your purpose plan.
8. Reflect on your work, save, display it, and share it with others.
9. Fix the root.
10. Get the fruit.

ACKNOWLEDGMENTS

To my family, friends, mentors, and clients, a thank you is not quite enough for the faith you've placed in me and the strength you've given me to continue this work. While I am passionate about helping businesses and leaders succeed, the root of that work is seeing other humans achieve. I've learned a lot over the years from reading, watching others, and interacting on all levels of life. Regardless of how I know you or where our paths may have crossed, I believe it was for a reason.

Thank you to those at Balboa Press and Hay House for continually pestering me to complete this book. Finishing this book in 2020, given the current landscape with COVID-19—earth's current pandemic—brings a fresh perspective to the timing of this publication and its global importance. I appreciate your guidance in the many edits, reviews, and publishing assistance.

Thank you to US Cellular Corporation and True North Companies for providing me the leadership and self-development opportunities to compile this manuscript of learning and a vision that is grounded in serving others. Fortune 500 raised me, but I believe entrepreneurship and writing this book have helped save me. I welcome all opportunities with any company looking to embed these learnings or share a full program for your employees into your training, development, wellness, and leadership programs.

To my team at Scoreboard Group Consulting, thanks for always being there for me and for being committed to the vision. Thousands of cups of coffee and networking went into building the ideas, thoughts, and documentation that were required to write and publish this book. I am excited about where we're going next and who will be coming along with us as we inspire others to fix the root and get the fruit!

Printed in the United States
By Bookmasters